D1710347

Danger on Apollo 13

THE GREAT ADVENTURES SERIES
Danger on Apollo 13

David Baker

Rourke Enterprises, Inc.
Vero Beach, Florida 32964

LIBRARY OF CONGRESS
Library of Congress Cataloging-in-Publication Data

Baker, David, 1944-
    Danger on Apollo 13/By David Baker.

    p. cm. — (Great adventures series)
    Includes index.
    Summary: Describes the trouble-plagued flight of
Apollo 13 in 1970, in which an explosion ended plans
for a lunar landing and forced the crew to embark on a
dangerous journey to return to Earth.
    ISBN 0-86592-871-1
    1. Apollo 13 (Spacecraft) — Juvenile literature.
2. Astronautics — Accidents 1970 — Juvenile literature.
[1. Apollo 13 (Spacecraft) 2. Astronautics—Accidents.]
I. Title.   II. Series:
TL793.B2344   1988   88-11365
629.45'4 - dc19   CIP
                                AC

Title page photo:

Bathed in light while preparations go on
for launch, Apollo 13 counts down to
lift-off.

CONTENTS

An Explosion In Space

"Okay 13, we've got Fred on TV."

At Mission Control in Houston the television sets flickered. Pictures of three men in a tiny space capsule were beamed to earth. Apollo 13 was transmitting an evening show to millions of people around the world. In Houston, it was 8:30 P.M. on Monday, April 13, 1970. Most people in Texas were sitting in their living rooms watching television, reading the papers, or getting home from a long day. In California, they were getting ready for bed, and in Hawaii most people were already asleep.

The astronauts had two spacecraft. One spacecraft was called *Odyssey*. The three astronauts lived in *Odyssey* all the way out and all the way back. The other spacecraft was called *Aquarius* and was built to land two astronauts on the moon. Both spacecraft would go into **moon orbit**, but only *Aquarius* would go down to the surface of the moon. *Aquarius* would remain attached to the front of *Odyssey* until it separated for the moon landing.

Apollo 13 had been in space for more than 55 hours when the TV show began 203,000 miles from earth. The spacecraft from which the TV picture was being broadcast was moving at 2,180 MPH. It would drift into the moon's **gravity** field several hours later and begin to speed up.

"What we plan to do for you today is start out in *Odyssey* and take

From a television camera aboard spacecraft Odyssey, a television camera sends pictures of Apollo 13 commander James B Lovell.

In the Mission Operations Control Room, NASA flight controllers monitor what started as an attempt at the nation's third man moon landing.

you on through from *Odyssey* into *Aquarius* and show you a little bit of the landing vehicle. Your TV operator is resting on the center couch, looking at Fred Haise, and Fred will now transport himself into the tunnel and into spaceship *Aquarius*."

From inside the spacecraft, TV pictures showed the crew floating weightless. They took earth watchers on a tour of *Odyssey* and then through the tunnel that separated *Odyssey* from *Aquarius*. It was only a black-and-white picture and it looked a little fuzzy. But to people on earth, flight controllers in Mission Control, and the families of the three astronauts, it was a welcome link with distant voyagers far from home. Within about 30 minutes, the TV show was over. It was time for the crew to go to sleep.

"This is the crew of Apollo 13 wishing everyone there a nice evening, and we're just about ready to close out our inspection of *Aquarius* and get back for a pleasant evening in *Odyssey*. Good night." The TV camera was switched off.

Suddenly, without warning, a loud bang shook the spacecraft.

Baja, California, is clearly seen in this stunning view from space as Apollo 13 heads for the moon.

Inside *Odyssey*, astronaut Jack Swigert was in the left couch, Jim Lovell was putting the TV camera away, and Fred Haise was closing the tunnel to the moon lander. Swigert spoke first. "Okay, Houston, we've had a problem." Warning bells were clanging and the instruments went wild. Something very serious had happened. It felt like an explosion. Could it be? Nobody had time to find out. Worse problems were on the way. Jim Lovell looked at the oxygen gauge. One of only two life-giving oxygen tanks was empty, and the second one was going down fast!

Oxygen from the one remaining tank also supplied three fuel cells, devices designed to produce electrical power for mixing oxygen with hydrogen. The hydrogen tank was all right, but without oxygen there was no means of producing electrical power. Without electricity in *Odyssey* there was no way of running life support equipment. And without oxygen, they would die anyway! Apollo 13 was on a course that would loop around the moon and fling *Odyssey* and *Aquarius* into deep space, never to return. What could they do?

From left to right, astronauts Swigert, Lovell, and Haise hold a model of the lunar module they planned to land on the moon and the Apollo spacecraft that would carry them to moon orbit.

The Mission of Apollo 13

Mission commander James B Lovell Jr had been in space several times since his first flight aboard Gemini VII in December 1965.

A lot of people were very worried about Apollo 13. Some superstitious people think the number 13 is bad luck. They said NASA should never have given the mission that number but should have moved straight from Apollo 12 to Apollo 14. Trying not to be superstitious itself, the space agency stuck with Apollo 13. Yet for all that, it did seem remarkably unlucky.

First, the mission was planned for as early as November, 1969. If Apollo 11 had been unable to make the first moon landing in July, 1969, NASA was prepared to try two more attempts that year. Apollo 12 as early as September and Apollo 13 in November. That would give three chances to fulfill the challenge set by President Kennedy to land men on the moon by the end of the 1960s.

When Apollo 11 was successful, Apollo 12 was postponed to November 1969, and Apollo 13 was planned for March 1970. Then that date was changed to April 11 to give more time for preparations. The crew had been chosen in August 1969. Jim Lovell would command Apollo 13. He had flown on the 14-day flight of Gemini 7 in December 1965. He had commanded Gemini 12 in November 1966. And he had been aboard the first moon orbit flight of Apollo 8 at Christmas 1968. Now, he would get to walk on the moon, or so he thought.

Lovell would occupy the left couch in spacecraft *Odyssey*. Next to him would be *Odyssey's* pilot, Ken Mattingly. On the far right couch would be Fred Haise. Both Mattingly and Haise would be making their first space flight. Mattingly would wait in *Odyssey* while Lovell and Haise went down to the moon for a 34-hour stay on the surface. During that time they were to have collected rocks on two moon walks.

On the morning of launch, a few hours before lift-off, the Apollo 13 crew eat a hearty breakfast with friends and colleagues at Cape Canaveral.

Even during preparation for flight, Apollo 13 seemed jinxed. While technicians cooled fuel pumps with liquid oxygen, they dumped clouds of oxygen into gullies. The gas rolled up the banks of the launch pad and set fire to police cars parked nearby! The concentrated oxygen made the running car engines ignite hot oil and grease.

Then, on the very day the countdown began, members of the crew were exposed to German measles. They could not risk becoming ill on a moon flight, although Lovell and Haise were checked by doctors and found to be immune to the illness. Ken Mattingly was not immune, and doctors would not know before launch day if he had caught it or not. They grounded him, and Jack Swigert took his place. There was a strange connection. The commander had only been selected because astronaut Mike Collins had to have an operation two years before, and his place had been taken by Lovell.

Nothing seemed right about Apollo 13. The equipment was troublesome, and two members of the crew were there directly or indirectly because of someone else's illness. Was the mission a jinxed flight? It seemed that way even as the launch took place. After lift-off, as the powerful **first stage** of the Saturn V rocket fell away, Apollo 13 nearly struck disaster. Vibrating violently, the center engine on the

While engineers and technicians prepare Apollo 13 and its Saturn V booster, space suit technicians get the Apollo 13 crew dressed for flight.

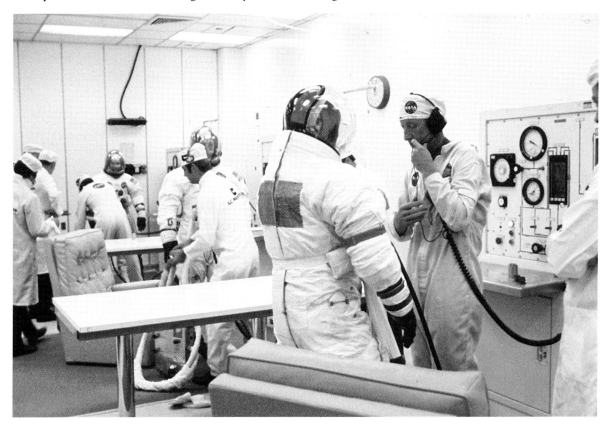

Lift-off! April 11, 1970, 2:13 P.M. EST.

second stage shut down far too early. The other four engines had to keep burning nearly a minute longer to compensate, and the third stage had to burn longer, too.

Finally, they boosted out of **earth orbit** toward the moon on a path that would loop them around the far side and fling them back to earth. After separating from the Saturn third stage, however, that path was changed. To reach the selected landing site, a place on the moon called Fra Mauro, they had to burn the main engine on *Odyssey* to change course. That firing took place less than 31 hours into the flight more than halfway to the moon. Apollo 13 was now committed to entering moon orbit. If left simply to loop around the moon on its new course it would never return to earth.

Keeping The Crew Alive

Odyssey had electrical power, food, water, and oxygen to keep three astronauts alive for at least two weeks. From launch to landing the entire mission had been planned to last ten days. During that time *Odyssey* would keep three men alive all the way to lunar orbit and back, and one man alive while his two colleagues went down to the moon. *Aquarius* had sufficient oxygen, food, and water for about 44 hours. Just enough to support two men for a moon landing and return to *Odyssey* in lunar orbit.

On the evening of April 13, 1970, all that had changed. The explosion aboard Apollo 13 had ripped out one of two oxygen tanks and damaged the second. The only remaining oxygen tank on *Odyssey* was leaking and would be empty within a few hours. After that, there would be no oxygen to breathe and no oxygen to produce electrical power. *Odyssey* would become a derelict capsule in the depths of space. Still attached to the moon lander *Aquarius*, it would skim the moon by 75 miles and be flung off into deep space by the moon's gravity.

Several hours earlier, the engine aboard *Odyssey* had been fired to

Housed inside its shroud at the top of the Saturn V third stage, the Lunar Module Aquarius will be extracted by the Apollo spacecraft Odyssey.

This artist's illustration shows how Odyssey moves back in to dock with Aquarius and pull it free of the Saturn V third stage.

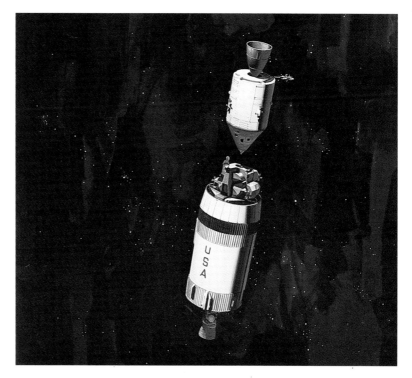

With bulky spacesuits on and lying in their couches for critical maneuvers of Odyssey and Aquarius, the Apollo 13 astronauts had little comfort on their way to the moon.

put Apollo 13 on course for lunar orbit. Now, the Apollo 13 astronauts knew they would not get to land on the moon. But that was the least of their worries. They did not even know if there was a way to save their lives. It was easy to panic, but that would only have made matters worse. The astronauts had trained for the day they would face almost certain death. Each one knew his survival would depend on remaining calm and trying to find a solution.

It seemed almost impossible. *Odyssey* was the only spacecraft that could get them back to earth and had a special heat shield to protect the capsule from very high temperatures on re-entering the earth's **atmosphere**. Parts of the spacecraft would glow red and reach 5,000 degrees Farenheit as it came back through the atmosphere. Before that could happen, the spacecraft had to get back on course, loop around the moon, and fly back across 240,000 miles of space. Yet only a couple of hours were left before the spacecraft ran out of oxygen and electrical power.

Aquarius was unable to carry the crew down through earth's atmosphere because it did not have a heat shield. It was built to operate only in space and on the airless moon. Yet it might be capable of keeping the crew alive when oxygen and power ran out in *Odyssey.* It was a tough challenge. *Aquarius* had been built to keep two men alive for 34 hours. Now, it would have to keep three men alive for nearly 100 hours. The only way for the crew to survive would be to use oxygen and electrical power from *Aquarius* and then climb into *Odyssey* for the final plunge through the atmosphere.

First things first. About 25 minutes after the explosion, with no alternative but to save their lives as long as possible, the crew began to think about using *Aquarius* as a lifeboat. They opened the hatch into the lunar lander and went inside. Back on earth the flight controllers were busy. They wanted to know exactly how long *Aquarius* could be made to keep the crew alive. All across the nation, the engineers who had built *Aquarius* got calls from Houston. How long would the water last? How could the power be turned down so it would last longer? What was the best way to make oxygen last? And how could Apollo 13 get back on course for earth?

Within a couple of hours, Lovell, Swigert, and Haise were in *Aquarius* with the hatch to *Odyssey* open. They had shut down all available systems in *Odyssey* and were breathing oxygen from the moon lander. For a few hours at least, the situation was stable. Plans were laid to get Apollo 13 back on earth-return course by firing the engine on *Aquarius.* Nobody knew if the big engine on *Odyssey* was damaged. Rocket motors can explode when damaged. *Aquarius* was not only a lifeboat, it was also a tug and would pull Apollo 13 back on course for earth.

The Apollo spacecraft called Odyssey was quite small and offered little room for moving around inside.

Around The Moon

It seems as though they are skimming the surface as Apollo 13 astronauts peer through the window to get the closest view they will obtain of the moon's craggy craters.

The crew had woken from their last sleep about 10:00 A.M. on the morning of April 13, 1970. Less than eleven hours later they were fighting for their lives. It would be a long time before they got rest again. Electrical power in *Odyssey* had been cut just before midnight, Houston time. For Apollo 13, April 13 had been a fateful day. Now it was time to prepare *Aquarius* to push the two spacecraft back on an earth-return course.

To do that the astronauts had to fire the engine on *Aquarius* that should have been used much later to land the crew on the moon. The firing took place at 2:44 A.M. in the early night hours of April 14 and lasted just 30 seconds. It changed the speed of Apollo 13 by just 26 MPH and shifted its flight path ever so slightly. Yet it was sufficient to move the path of Apollo 13 from a close miss around the moon of 75 miles to 158 miles. The slight change in course would allow the gravity of the moon to throw Apollo 13 around from the far side back toward earth. Minor corrections would be needed later to put it precisely on track.

For the first time since the explosion, the crew had been able to do something positive about getting home. They had used *Aquarius* not only to save their lives but to put them on an earth-return path. Now it was time to see if the water, oxygen, and electrical power available in *Aquarius* would last. Calculations showed it would be close.

On their present course, the crew of Apollo 13 would reach earth almost four days after they fired the engine on *Aquarius*. At the present rate they were using it, the water supply would run out in two days! Water was not only used for drinking. As far as getting back to earth was concerned, the most important use was for cooling the systems in *Aquarius*. Without cooling, electrical equipment in the

Getting bigger and bigger as they fall toward it, Apollo 13 astronauts get fleeting glimpses of the moon as each hour sends them closer and closer towards their objective.

spacecraft would overheat and stop working within an hour or so. They would need to make big savings to keep the spacecraft operating.

The oxygen supply was not a real problem. There would be quite enough to last four days. This was because *Aquarius* carried much more than it needed for crew survival. On the moon, as intended, the cabin supply of oxygen would normally have been vented to space so the crew could open the hatch and get out in their moon suits. After getting back in again the cabin would have been filled with oxygen like water in a bath tub. Without landing on the moon and venting oxygen for a moon walk, there would be sufficient oxygen for all three astronauts on the journey back to earth.

Worst of all was electrical power. The crew tried to turn off as much equipment as possible to save the batteries. *Odyssey* had fuel cells that produced electricity as long as oxygen and hydrogen were fed in. Those were now useless. *Aquarius* had batteries that would not continue to provide power when they ran down. To last all the way back, the crew had to use less power than engineers calculated was the absolute minimum to keep the crew alive. There was barely enough supply to last the return journey.

Because of this, flight controllers decided to speed up Apollo 13 by

Across a crater called Tsiolkovsky, the astronauts catch a breathtaking view of the scene below.

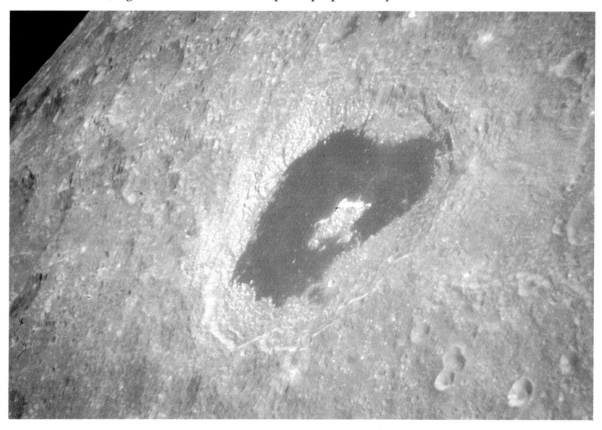

about half a day. But first, the flight path would carry the crew around the far side of the moon. They were out of sight from the earth for a nail-biting twenty-five minutes. As Jim Lovell, Fred Haise, and Jack Swigert came around the moon they looked down at the rocks, the craters, and the boulders far below. It looked so close they felt they could touch the surface. In fact, Apollo 13 came no closer than 158 miles. Jim Lovell had been here before when he made the first historic journey to moon orbit on Christmas Eve 1968. On that day he had read verses from the Bible telling how God created earth, the moon, and the stars. Now all three astronauts aboard Apollo 13 were praying for their lives.

The crew had hoped to take detailed pictures of the lunar surface with a special topographic camera attached to the window of their tiny spacecraft.

The Long Journey

Apollo 13 had been flung around the moon like a stone from a slingshot. The spacecraft was now on its way back to earth. It would take more than three days to reach home, but that was too long. Batteries would not last three days, and water to cool equipment would run out. Something had to be done to speed up the capsule. The astronauts would have to fire a rocket motor to increase speed by nearly 600 MPH. This would cut nearly ten hours off the journey home and would give them a real chance to make it back before the spacecraft gave out.

About two hours after passing behind the moon, Jim Lovell and Fred Haise got ready to fire the big rocket engine on *Aquarius*. They kept it burning for more than four minutes. When it finally shut down, the engine had increased the speed of Apollo 13 by 586 MPH. The spacecraft was scheduled to splash down in the Pacific Ocean two days and fifteen hours later. Until then, they would be tracked by flight controllers in Mission Control. Information to put them exactly on course would be gathered by tracking stations around the world. Tiny course corrections could be made using the smaller rocket motors on *Aquarius*.

As yet, nobody had given much thought to what had caused the explosion. All attention had been on getting the crew back alive. But now flight controllers at NASA's Johnson Space Center near Houston began to worry. Suppose something had gone wrong with the heat shield on *Odyssey*. There was no way of knowing if it had been affected by the explosion or not. Only the hot ride down through the atmosphere would tell. And now there was another problem. The crew might have enough oxygen to breathe, but they might be gassed to death by poisonous carbon dioxide.

Tense hours in Mission Control keep flight controllers riveted to their consoles, monitoring every step of the way back home for the crew of Apollo 13.

This pre-flight shot of Fred Haise in the Aquarius simulator shows how little room was available in the spacecraft that became their lifeboat back to earth.

On earth, when we breathe, we take in oxygen and give out carbon dioxide. Carbon dioxide is poisonous if it builds up in the human system. The atmosphere distributes it, and plants breathe in carbon dioxide to produce oxygen. In Apollo there were no plants to re-cycle the carbon dioxide Lovell, Swigert, and Haise exhaled. If carbon dioxide levels increased above a certain level, the crew would be poisoned and die. On a normal flight, special filters trapped the gas and prevented it from poisoning the crew. The filters were in canisters, and each canister had to be changed every few hours. The canisters in *Aquarius* would not last long enough to get the crew back to earth, and the canisters in *Odyssey* would not fit the oxygen system in *Aquarius*!

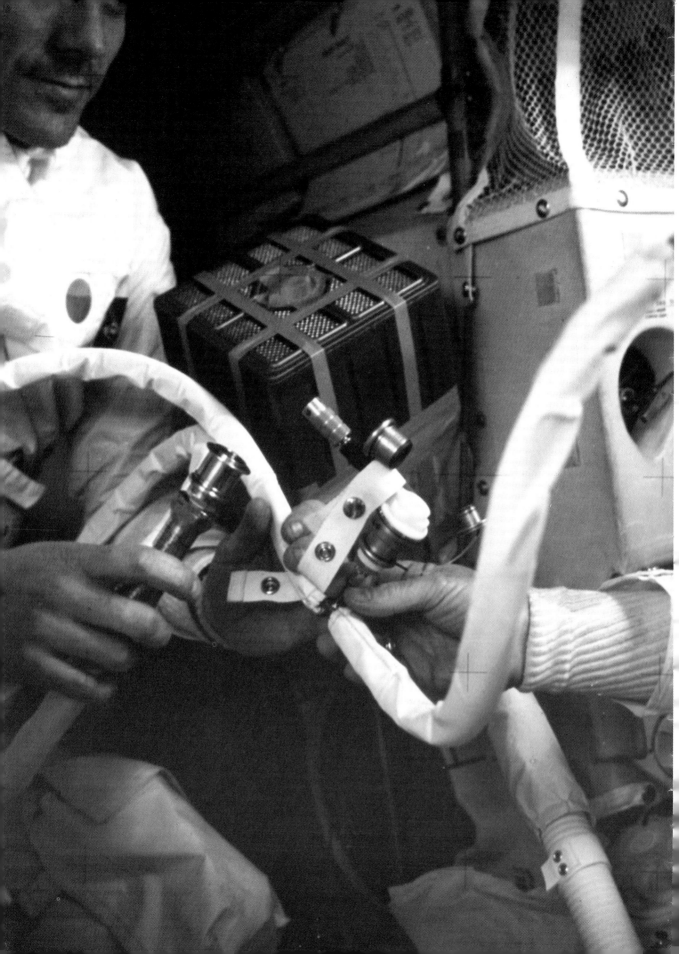

Using tape and hoses, the crew successfully lash up the makeshift device that will prevent them being poisoned by their own exhaled breath.

Using adhesive tape and cardboard, flight controllers devised a way to fix the filter boxes from *Odyssey* on to the hoses from *Aquarius*. They tried it out on earth and it seemed to work. Now the crew had to do it inside their tiny living area to keep the level of poisonous gas down below the danger levels. Because Apollo 13 was limping home in a crippled condition, flight controllers wanted at least one of the crew awake at all times. This was different from their normal procedure, where all three astronauts on Apollo flights slept at the same time. About seventeen hours after he last slept, Fred Haise tried to get some rest. Six hours later he woke, and all three men had a meal as best they could. Then, twenty-four hours after Lovell and Swigert had been able to sleep, they too began a six-hour rest.

Inside the darkened spacecraft, Fred Haise lay watching the few lights that remained on board Apollo 13. It was getting colder. Jim Lovell and Jack Swigert tried to sleep but kept waking up. It was an eerie feeling. They had deliberately switched off systems never intended to stop working on a space flight. They were still alive almost a full day after the explosion. Was there still some unknown danger lurking aboard Apollo 13? No one knew, and the greatest risks still lay ahead.

Carbon dioxide absorber cans from Odyssey are brought to Aquarius and adapted to fit the equipment in their lifeboat spacecraft.

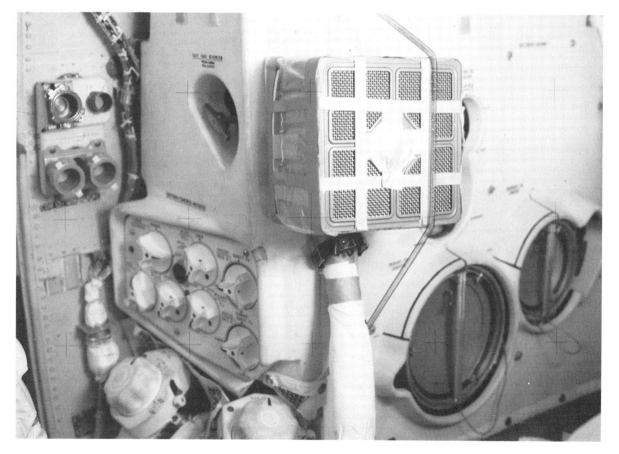

Home

Although supposed to get a full six hours sleep, Jim Lovell was up and about after less than three hours. He was soon joined by Jack Swigert. They had spent the first full day after the explosion going around the moon, speeding up the return journey, and staying alive. The second day would be spent fixing all the carbon dioxide filters with tape, cardboard, and prayers. At the end of that day, Wednesday, April 15, *Aquarius* passed the halfway point in its role as a lifeboat.

Because *Odyssey* was lifeless and all oxygen and what little heat could be provided came from *Aquarius*, conditions in *Odyssey* were getting worse. *Aquarius* creaked and groaned as temperatures fell lower and lower. When talking to astronaut Deke Slayton in Mission Control, Jack Swigert was concerned about sleeping in *Odyssey*. "I'll tell you, Deke, it's cold up in there. I don't know whether we'll be able to sleep up there tonight. It must be 35 or 40 degrees." The next two days would seem like weeks.

At one point the crew fired tiny thrusters on *Aquarius* to put them on a more precise course for home. But there was little else to do as a way of breaking the boredom. Suddenly, an indication in Mission Control that one of *Aquarius's* batteries had failed sent shivers of alarm. Without both batteries working all the way back, the crew would be dead on arrival. Quick checks showed it was a faulty indicator.

It was now getting very cold. The crew put on their moon boots, then their gloves, and finally any other piece of clothing they could find. Sleep became impossible. They dozed crouched together for warmth, in corners and away from the walls. The temperature was

This fuzzy photograph taken by the Apollo 13 crew of the large service module separated just before re-entry, shows a complete panel just above the rocket engine blown away by the explosion of an oxygen module many hours before. This was the first glimpse this crew got of how close they came to total disaster.

Through a cloud-filled sky appears the heartwarming sight for ground-based flight controllers as three large parachutes gently lower the command module of spacecraft Odyssey through the atmosphere toward the sea.

almost down to the freezing point. Moisture gathered on the walls, and water began to trickle down the windows and into cables and instrument panels. The food lockers felt like refrigerators. The tension was taking its toll. From Mission Control came a cruel question: "Is it snowing in *Odyssey* yet?"

Around the nation and across the world people prayed and stopped work to listen to the voices of three men struggling back to earth. Their voices crackled and were difficult to hear because the radio transmitters were turned as low as possible to save electrical power. The hours went by slowly. In space, Lovell, Haise, and Swigert could do nothing but huddle together for warmth and nibble chilled food to keep their strength up. Mission Control encouraged them. "Hang in there. It won't be long."

And then there was something to work for. As earth came nearer and nearer, the crew had to feed the last of *Aquarius's* battery power into *Odyssey* so it could safely return them through the atmosphere. In Houston it was the early hours of Friday, April 17, the day Apollo 13 would return. As dawn broke across the Texas panhandle, a

The command module of spacecraft Odyssey is lifted aboard the carrier that earlier had retrieved the astronauts from the sea.

cheerful cry came from space. "Hey, it's warmed up here now.... I'm looking out the window now and that earth is whistling in like a high-speed freight train."

One last course correction was made, and then the astronauts gathered in *Odyssey*, now using the last of its juice. The big service module, where an oxygen tank had exploded three days before, was cut loose. As it drifted away, they peered through the window looking for signs of damage. From Jim Lovell came a chilling comment on what all three astronauts saw for the first time. "There's one whole side of that spacecraft missing. The whole panel is blown out."

Now it was time to cut *Aquarius* loose. It would plunge through the atmosphere and burn up. "Goodbye, *Aquarius*, and we thank you", was the affectionate call from space. Only eight hours of power and twelve hours of water remained. It had been a close call. Thirty-five minutes later, *Odyssey* brought all three astronauts safely back through the atmosphere to thunderous applause from Mission Control. It had been a fantastic race for survival, and they had won.

Their lives saved, three happy astronauts walk from the helicopter that retrieved them, breathing fresh air for the first time in several days.

Glossary

Atmosphere	The layer of air surrounding the earth.
Earth Orbit	A circular path traveled around the earth.
First Stage	The bottom section of a rocket which houses the engines that provide the initial lift-off thrust. This stage usually fires for between two and four minutes and is then separated to allow the upper stages to ignite in turn.
Gravity	A planet or star's pull or force of attraction that gives objects weight. Outside the earth's gravity, people and objects become weightless.
Moon Orbit	A circular path traveled around the moon.

Index